POP SONGS

IN A

CLASSICAL

STYLE

Arranged by David Pearl

ISBN 978-1-70513-156-5

Visit Hal Leonard Online at
www.halleonard.com

Contact us:
Hal Leonard
7777 West Bluemound Road
Milwaukee, WI 53213
Email: info@halleonard.com

In Europe, contact:
Hal Leonard Europe Limited
42 Wigmore Street
Marylebone, London, W1U 2RN
Email: info@halleonardeurope.com

In Australia, contact:
Hal Leonard Australia Pty. Ltd.
4 Lentara Court
Cheltenham, Victoria, 3192 Australia
Email: info@halleonard.com.au

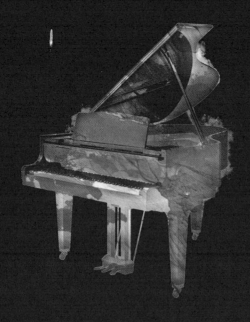

AIN'T NO SUNSHINE

Words and Music by
BILL WITHERS

BLACKBIRD

Words and Music by JOHN LENNON
and PAUL McCARTNEY

DON'T STOP BELIEVIN'

Words and Music by STEVE PERRY,
NEAL SCHON and JONATHAN CAIN

D.S. al Coda
(with repeat)

CODA

DREAM ON

Words and Music by
STEVEN TYLER

DUST IN THE WIND

Words and Music by
KERRY LIVGREN

Moderately, flowing

With pedal

To Coda ⊕

FROM A DISTANCE

Words and Music by
JULIE GOLD

GOD ONLY KNOWS

Words and Music by BRIAN WILSON
and TONY ASHER

HERO

Words and Music by MARIAH CAREY
and WALTER AFANASIEFF

KISS FROM A ROSE

Words and Music by
HENRY OLUSEGUN ADEOLA SAMUEL

Moderately slow, in 2

MAD WORLD

Words and Music by
ROLAND ORZABAL

SAY MY NAME

Words and Music by BEYONCÉ KNOWLES,
KELENDRIA ROWLAND, RODNEY JERKINS,
LaSHAWN DANIELS, FRED JERKINS,
LaTAVIA ROBERSON and LeTOYA LUCKETT

41

SWEET CHILD O' MINE

Words and Music by W. AXL ROSE,
SLASH, IZZY STRADLIN',
DUFF McKAGAN and STEVEN ADLER

D.S. al Coda

CODA

Faster, driving beat

poco accel.

TIME IN A BOTTLE

Words and Music by
JIM CROCE

UP, UP AND AWAY

Words and Music by
JIMMY WEBB

Moderately, freely moving

With pedal

WHAT'S LOVE GOT TO DO WITH IT

Words and Music by GRAHAM LYLE
and TERRY BRITTEN

YOU CAN'T HURRY LOVE

Words and Music by EDWARD HOLLAND JR.,
LAMONT DOZIER and BRIAN HOLLAND

Moderately bright, steady

mp staccato

Creative PIANO SOLO

Looking to add some variety to your playing? Enjoy these beautifully distinctive arrangements for piano solo! These popular tunes get new and unique treatments for a fun and fresh presentation. Explore new styles and enjoy these favorites with a bit of a twist! Each collection includes 20 songs for the intermediate to advanced player.

BOHEMIAN RHAPSODY & OTHER EPIC SONGS
Band on the Run • A Day in the Life • Free Bird • November Rain • Piano Man • Roundabout • Stairway to Heaven • Take the Long Way Home • and more.

00196019 Piano Solo.................................**$14.99**

CHRISTMAS CAROLS
Away in a Manger • Deck the Hall • The First Noel • God Rest Ye Merry, Gentlemen • Hark! the Herald Angels Sing • It Came upon the Midnight Clear • Jingle Bells • Joy to the World • O Holy Night • Silent Night • Up on the Housetop • We Three Kings of Orient Are • What Child Is This? • and more.

00147214 Piano Solo **$14.99**

CHRISTMAS COLLECTION
Blue Christmas • The Christmas Song (Chestnuts Roasting on an Open Fire) • Frosty the Snow Man • Here Comes Santa Claus (Right down Santa Claus Lane) • Let It Snow! Let It Snow! Let It Snow! • Silver Bells • Sleigh Ride • White Christmas • Winter Wonderland • and more.

00172042 Piano Solo **$14.99**

CLASSIC ROCK
Another One Bites the Dust • Aqualung • Beast of Burden • Born to Be Wild • Carry on Wayward Son • Layla • Owner of a Lonely Heart • Roxanne • Smoke on the Water • Sweet Emotion • Takin' It to the Streets • 25 or 6 to 4 • Welcome to the Jungle • and more!

00138517 Piano Solo **$14.99**

Prices, contents, and availability subject to change without notice.

DISNEY FAVORITES
Beauty and the Beast • Can You Feel the Love Tonight • Chim Chim Cher-ee • For the First Time in Forever • How Far I'll Go • Let It Go • Mickey Mouse March • Remember Me (Ernesto de la Cruz) • You'll Be in My Heart • You've Got a Friend in Me • and more.

00283318 Piano Solo................................**$14.99**

JAZZ POP SONGS
Don't Know Why • I Just Called to Say I Love You • I Put a Spell on You • Just the Way You Are • Killing Me Softly with His Song • Mack the Knife • Michelle • Smooth Operator • Sunny • Take Five • What a Wonderful World • and more.

00195426 Piano Solo................................**$14.99**

JAZZ STANDARDS
All the Things You Are • Beyond the Sea • Georgia on My Mind • In the Wee Small Hours of the Morning • The Lady Is a Tramp • Like Someone in Love • A Nightingale Sang in Berkeley Square • Someone to Watch Over Me • That's All • What'll I Do? • and more.

00283317 Piano Solo................................**$14.99**

POP BALLADS
Against All Odds (Take a Look at Me Now) • Bridge over Troubled Water • Fields of Gold • Hello • I Want to Know What Love Is • Imagine • In Your Eyes • Let It Be • She's Got a Way • Total Eclipse of the Heart • You Are So Beautiful • Your Song • and more.

00195425 Piano Solo................................**$14.99**

POP HITS
Billie Jean • Fields of Gold • Get Lucky • Happy • Ho Hey • I'm Yours • Just the Way You Are • Let It Go • Poker Face • Radioactive • Roar • Rolling in the Deep • Royals • Smells like Teen Spirit • Viva la Vida • Wonderwall • and more.

00138156 Piano Solo................................**$14.99**

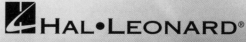

www.halleonard.com